Of Mice and Men

Lightbox Literature Studies

Piper Whelan

LIGHTBOX
openlightbox.com

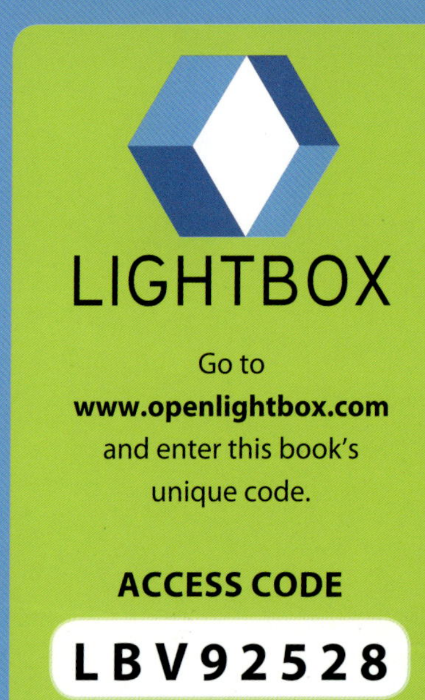

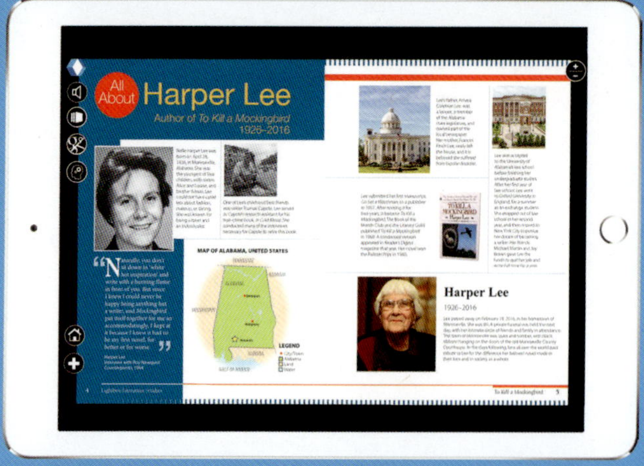

Lightbox is an all-inclusive digital solution for the teaching and learning of curriculum topics in an original, groundbreaking way. Lightbox is based on National Curriculum Standards.

STANDARD FEATURES OF LIGHTBOX

AUDIO High-quality narration using text-to-speech system

VIDEOS Embedded high-definition video clips

ACTIVITIES Printable PDFs that can be emailed and graded

WEBLINKS Curated links to external, child-safe resources

SLIDESHOWS Pictorial overviews of key concepts

TRANSPARENCIES Step-by-step layering of maps, diagrams, charts, and timelines

INTERACTIVE MAPS Interactive maps and aerial satellite imagery

QUIZZES Ten multiple choice questions that are automatically graded and emailed for teacher assessment

KEY WORDS Matching key concepts to their definitions

MORE Extra information and details on the subject

FIRST HAND Letters, diaries, and other primary sources

DOCS Speeches, newspaper articles, and other historical documents

Contents

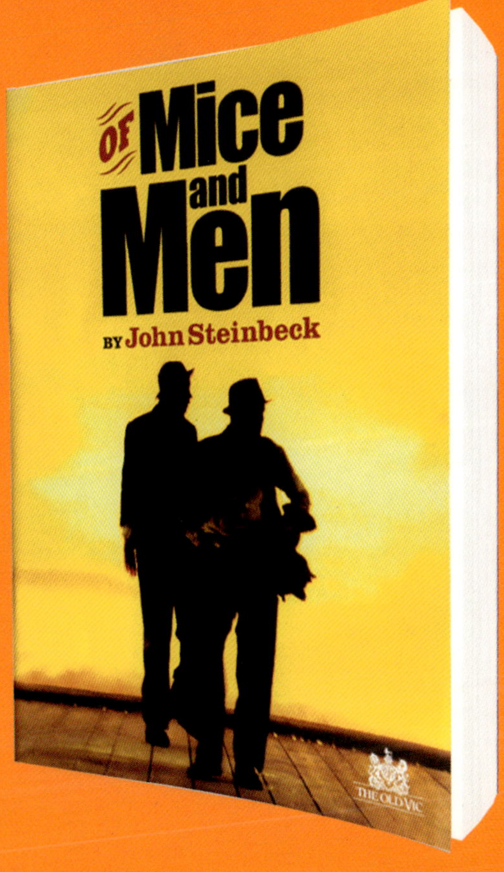

2 Access Lightbox Student Edition
4 All About John Steinbeck
6 Setting of the Novella
8 Time Period of the Novella
10 Conflict in the Novella
12 Introducing the Characters
14 The Art of Storytelling
16 Theme in the Novella
18 Symbolism in the Novella
20 The Use of Language
22 Impact of the Novella at the Time of Publishing
24 Impact of the Novella Now
26 Perspectives on Disabilities and Inclusion
28 Writing a Comparative Essay
30 Key Words/Literary Terms
31 Index
32 Log on to www.openlightbox.com

EXTENSION ACTIVITY

Researching for a Writing Assignment

Students will complete a thorough research process to prepare for a writing assignment, and organize their research in a logical manner that supports their writing. An exemplary research process will meet the following criteria.

- Creates a goal for the research, based on the topic and working thesis
- Creates specific, thoughtful, and inventive research questions that are relevant to the topic of the writing assignment
- Produces a list of categories, key words, and related ideas to effectively assist in researching
- Uses high-quality sources that pertain to the topic and come in a variety of formats, such as books, journals, primary sources, websites, and databases
- Determines accuracy of all sources
- Uses sources that provide balanced research and various perspectives on the topic in question
- Takes notes to highlight the key facts and ideas in order to answer all research questions
- Extracts relevant, detailed information from the sources during the note-taking process
- Organizes the research notes in a clear and concise manner
- Organizes the research notes logically and in a way that sets up the information and ideas for analysis and the writing process
- Analyzes the information and produces ideas and points to support the working thesis
- Uses an effective and suitable format to present all research
- Properly cites all sources used

John Steinbeck

Author of *Of Mice and Men*
1902–1968

John Ernst Steinbeck Jr. was born on February 27, 1902, in Salinas, California. His father, John Ernst Steinbeck Sr., worked a number of jobs, including managing a flour mill and running his own feed store, while his mother, Olive Hamilton Steinbeck, was a schoolteacher. Steinbeck had three sisters. As a child, he was described as smart and shy, and spent much of his childhood writing stories and poems.

> **"If there is a magic in story writing, and I am convinced there is, no one has ever been able to reduce it to a recipe that can be passed from one person to another. The formula seems to lie solely in the aching urge of the writer to convey something he feels important to the reader."**
>
> John Steinbeck
>
> Excerpt from a Letter to Edith Mirrielees, 1962
> Published in *The Paris Review*, 1975

MAP OF CALIFORNIA, UNITED STATES

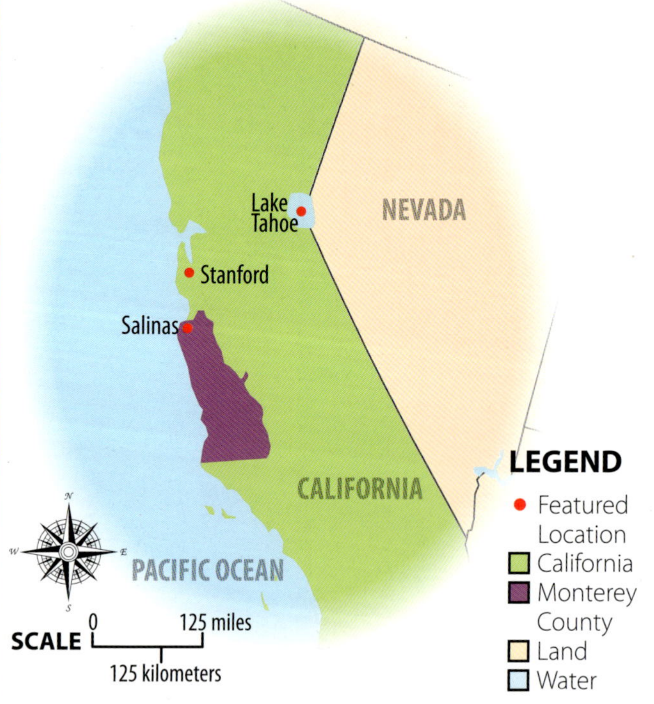

Steinbeck began post-secondary studies in 1919 at Stanford University in California. He attended sporadically for six years and dropped out in 1925 without earning a degree. Steinbeck then moved to New York City, where he worked as a newspaper reporter and as a construction worker before eventually returning to California to focus on his writing.

While working as the caretaker of an estate at Lake Tahoe, Steinbeck wrote his first novella, *Cup of Gold*. Published in 1929, it was followed by his next two novellas, *The Pastures of Heaven* and *To a God Unknown*. None of these three books was commercially successful. Steinbeck became well-known when *Tortilla Flat*, a collection of warm, humorous stories, was published in 1935.

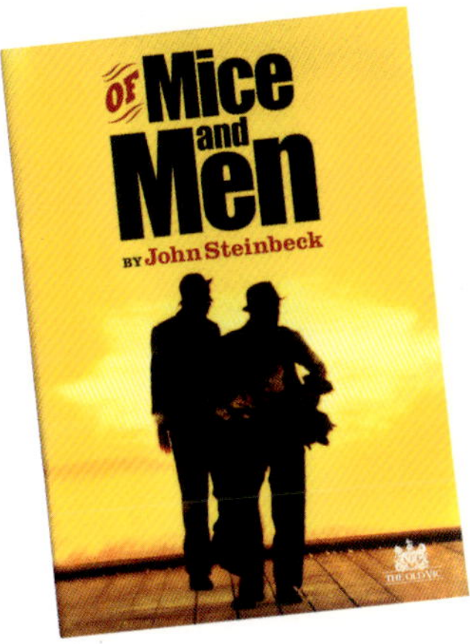

Steinbeck's writings during the 1930s were more serious than his earlier works. In 1937, Steinbeck published his **novella**, *Of Mice and Men*. This story is considered one of his best works. In 1939, Steinbeck published another classic, *The Grapes of Wrath*, which won a Pulitzer Prize.

Steinbeck wrote 16 novellas, as well as screenplays, short stories, essays, plays, and travel narratives. During World War II, he worked as a war correspondent for the *New York Herald Tribune*. His best-known works in his later years include *East of Eden, Cannery Row*, and *The Winter of Our Discontent*. Steinbeck died on December 20, 1968, in New York City.

TEACHER NOTES

Google Maps

132 Central Ave,
Salinas, California

Explore John Steinbeck's boyhood home, which is now a restaurant and gift shop, using the street view of his neighborhood.

Weblink

John Steinbeck's *Tortilla Flat* Is Not for 'Literary Slummers'

Examine Jordison's article in *The Guardian* about Steinbeck's first commercially successful book.

1. What do you think Steinbeck means by the term "literary slummers"? How fair is this phrase? How warranted is his offense to the public's response?
2. Imagine you are the author of a book about one of your family members. The public response to this characterization of your family member is not pleasant. How would you react? What reasons do you have for your response? Write an open letter in response to the public.

EXTENSION ACTIVITY

Analyzing a Newspaper Article

Students will assess a newspaper article and write an analysis. An exemplary analysis will meet the following criteria.

- Identifies the topic of the article
- Identifies the main points and opinions presented in the article
- Identifies the writer of the article
- Presents information about the writer and infers how his or her life may have shaped this opinion
- Assesses the writer's reliability
- Analyzes how the writer makes his or her argument
- Uses evidence from the article to show how the writer supports his or her argument
- Analyzes the writer's use of literary devices to enhance the article
- Differentiates between the facts and opinions presented in the article
- Identifies when and where the article was published, and determines its intended audience
- Identifies and understands the goals of the article
- Assesses the effectiveness of the format (a newspaper opinion article) in presenting the writer's argument
- Connects the article to the societal and historical context in which it was written
- Infers what is not said about this topic in the article
- Identifies what information is unintentionally implied in the article
- Infers what other opinions may be presented about this topic and who may be most likely to express them
- Uses a number of other resources to analyze the context of the article

Setting of the Novella

Many of Steinbeck's novellas are set in his home state of California. The Salinas Valley, where he was raised, and the Pacific Coast, where he spent summers with his family, were especially important to him. *Of Mice and Men* is set on a ranch near Soledad, California, just south of Steinbeck's hometown. In a letter to George Albee, Steinbeck wrote, "I think I would like to write the story of this whole valley, of all the little towns and all the farms and the ranches in the wilder hills. I can see how I would like to do it so that it would be the valley of the world."

The Salinas Valley

"A few miles south of Soledad, the Salinas River drops in close to the hillside bank and runs deep and green. The water is warm too, for it has slipped twinkling over the yellow sands in the sunlight before reaching the narrow pool. On one side of the river the golden foothill slopes curve up to the strong and rocky Gabilan mountains, but on the valley side the water is lined with trees—willows fresh and green with every spring, carrying in their lower leaf junctures the debris of the winter's flooding; and sycamore with mottled, white, recumbent limbs and branches that arch over the pool. On the sandy bank under the trees the leaves lie deep and so crisp that a lizard makes a great skittering if he runs among them."

Chapter 1

The California ranch in *Of Mice and Men* is based on the farms and ranches where Steinbeck worked as a student. As a manual laborer, he worked with **itinerant** agricultural workers and learned about their everyday lives. The early history of the city of Soledad was shaped by agriculture, particularly beef and dairy cattle, wheat, and barley production in the nineteenth century. In the 1920s, row crop technology brought new farming opportunities to the area, increasing the number of migrant workers coming to Soledad.

In *Of Mice and Men*, George and Lennie hope to build a new life by buying their own farm. This was a dream shared by migrants who left the Great Plains states in the 1930s seeking better times in California. However, life in California was not what they had hoped. Jobs were scarce, and many farms were owned by companies. Workers were usually paid meager wages based on the amount of fruit they picked, and they often had to rent run-down shacks and buy expensive groceries from their employer's stores.

TEACHER NOTES

Weblink

Steinbeck Country Tour
Examine the article from San José State University discussing the California locales depicted in Steinbeck's fiction.

1. How is Steinbeck's view that humans and nature are connected reflected in his works? What parallels can be drawn between the land and the characters in *Of Mice and Men*?
2. How might familiarity with real places lend itself to more compelling writing? In what ways might knowledge of people or places hinder fictional writing about it? Provide explanations for your ideas.

First Hand

Letters From the Dust Bowl
Analyze these letters written by a woman living in Oklahoma during the Dust Bowl in the 1930s.

1. What factors led people to move west? Was the move to California worth it for migrants in the long run? Why or why not?
2. How would you describe the attitude and tone of the letters? Does the writer seem hopeful, discouraged, or a mix of the two? Provide evidence for your ideas.
3. How might an event such as the Dust Bowl unfold during the present day economy and political climate? What effect would it have on the United States as a whole?

EXTENSION ACTIVITY

Conducting an Interview

Students will conduct an interview with a community member about a time period in their community's history, and submit an audio recording and transcript of the interview. An exemplary interview will meet the following criteria.

- Clearly defines the purpose of the interview
- Conducts thorough background research to inform the focus of the interview and the questions
- Drafts a complete list of thoughtful, in-depth, and varied questions prior to the interview
- Interviews a subject with relevant knowledge on the topic and time period in question
- Asks questions in a logical order, building upon each other
- Treats the interview subject in a polite, respectful, and professional manner
- Does not interrupt or rush the interview subject
- Shows interest and enthusiasm in responses and follow-up questions
- Chooses follow-up questions that demonstrate active listening
- Asks for clarification and further details when necessary
- Asks questions about personal experiences related to the topic
- Asks questions regarding factual information and the interview subject's opinion on the topic
- Asks creative questions that reflect fresh insights on the topic
- Records the full interview in a quiet environment
- Organizes and edits the interview transcript to be clear and factual

Time Period of the Novella

Of Mice and Men was set in the 1930s, an era defined by the Great Depression. This setting provides the backdrop for Steinbeck's empathy for laborers and his views on **social justice** for workers. Steinbeck captures the experience of the itinerant worker in his novella, as well as the dream of a better life.

Snapshot

Migrant Workers in the 1930s

In 1933, the **wage** earned by **California migrant workers** dropped from **35** to **17** cents per hour.

2.5 million people **left the Great Plains** states to escape the Dust Bowl.

About **40 percent** of all **migrant workers** came to California's **San Joaquin Valley**.

Itinerant Workers

"I seen hundreds of men come by on the road an' on the ranches, with their bundles on their backs an' that same [expletive] thing in their heads. … Hundreds of them. They come, an' they quit an' go on; an' every [expletive] one of 'em's got a little piece of land in his head. An' never a [expletive] one of 'em ever gets it. Just like heaven. Ever'body wants a little piece of lan'. I read plenty of books out here. Nobody never gets to heaven, and nobody gets no land. . . . It's just in their head."

Crooks, Chapter 4

The Great Depression was a global economic crisis that resulted from the 1929 stock market crash. The price of wheat fell drastically. Drought and violent windstorms turned the Great Plains into what became known as the Dust Bowl, destroying crops and killing livestock. Poverty and high unemployment rates across the United States lasted through the next decade. Unemployed workers filled job lines and soup kitchens, and homeless families built shelters of salvaged materials.

In 1936, Steinbeck wrote several articles on migrant farm workers for the *San Francisco News*. In the process of writing these articles, Steinbeck got an in-depth look at the lives led by these workers, who were often members of ethnic minorities. While there had been itinerant workers in the United States for decades, the Great Depression resulted in an increase in migrant workers, and worsened the conditions they faced. In 1937—the year *Of Mice and Men* was published—an estimated 200,000 to 350,000 itinerant workers wandered the country.

TEACHER NOTES

Weblink

Survivors Of The Great Depression Tell Their Stories
Examine the accounts of individuals who lived through the Great Depression.

1. How do the subjects of the interviews portray their experience of the Great Depression? On which aspects of life do they focus? Why might they focus on these areas?
2. How did the Great Depression affect their lives? What factors influenced this effect?
3. How do the experiences of the interviewees compare to one another? What might have influenced any differences in their lives during this period?

Document

Article V of *The Harvest Gypsies*
Study Steinbeck's account of the plight of migrant families from a book of articles first published in 1936 in the *San Francisco News*.

1. Compare and contrast the diets of migrants making money with the diets of the poor of modern America. How different are their diets? What might be the reasons for this?
2. Research the kinds of social assistance available for the poor in the 1930s and compare it with welfare programs offered in the United States today. What are the benefits and drawbacks of each? Where has the United States improved its programs? What improvements still need to be made?

EXTENSION ACTIVITY

Writing a Short Story

Students will choose an excerpt from the novella and use it as their inspiration in writing a short story. An exemplary short story will meet the following criteria.

- Engages the reader from the opening line
- Establishes a clear, consistent point of view
- Introduces a narrator and a setting
- Develops an engaging conflict at the heart of the narrative to build tension and keep the reader interested
- Develops characters and events through purposeful and well-crafted literary devices
- Creates a logical progression of events in the narrative that build upon each other using various techniques
- Explores ideas, concepts, and writing styles with creativity and originality
- Demonstrates a high level of skill in using appropriate narrative techniques to tell the story
- Concludes the narrative in a thoughtful, effective manner appropriate to the narrative
- Uses varied, purposeful diction and syntax to affect style and serve the narrative
- Writes with clarity, imagination, and a unique, personal voice
- Does not use stereotypes or clichés
- Uses effective, believable dialogue
- Uses correct spelling, grammar, and punctuation

Conflict in the Novella

In literature, conflict is a struggle between two or more opposing forces, creating a tension that must be resolved. This is the main challenge that the protagonist faces throughout the story. This struggle is often between the protagonist and antagonist, but there are other types of conflict found in literature. Conflict is a vital element in any piece of literature. Without it, there is no story.

The Four Major Types of Conflict in Literature

CHARACTER vs. CHARACTER

The protagonist struggles against an opposing character, usually the antagonist. This is a common type of conflict in fiction. In the 1986 film *Top Gun*, Maverick, a pilot in the U.S. Navy's Fighter Weapons School, develops a rivalry with another pilot, Iceman, who resents Maverick's dangerous behavior.

CHARACTER vs. SELF

The protagonist fights an inner battle with himself or herself. The battle is often about a major decision he or she has to make. In *The Great Gatsby*, Jay Gatsby believes he can win back his lost love, Daisy Buchanan. He recreates himself but is blinded by dreams he is unable to fulfill.

CHARACTER vs. SOCIETY

The protagonist is opposed to the principles or actions of his or her community or society as a whole. This conflict is based upon the protagonist's beliefs. In *Nineteen Eighty-Four*, Winston Smith rebels against the Party and its all-seeing leader, Big Brother. He writes his true feelings about society and becomes involved with a resistance organization.

CHARACTER vs. NATURE

The protagonist faces an obstacle or challenge in nature. This may be an entire landscape or a symbolic representation of nature, such as an animal or natural disaster. In *127 Hours*, mountain climber Aron Ralston has his arm crushed by a falling boulder, trapping him in a Utah canyon. In the ensuing days, Ralston struggles to overcome his injuries and stay alive.

Types of Conflict in *Of Mice and Men*

The three main types of conflict in *Of Mice and Men* are character versus character, character versus self, and character versus society.

Character versus Character

"'If he tangles with you, Lennie, we're gonna get the can. Don't make no mistake about that. He's the boss's son. Look, Lennie. You try to keep away from him, will you? Don't never speak to him. If he comes in here you move clear to the other side of the room. Will you do that, Lennie?' 'I don't want no trouble,' Lennie mourned. 'I never done nothing to him.'"

George Milton and Lennie Small, Chapter 2

Character versus Self

"Lennie said, 'I thought you was mad at me, George.' 'No,' said George. 'No, Lennie. I ain't mad. I never been mad, an' I ain't now. That's a thing I want ya to know.'"

Lennie Small and George Milton, Chapter 6

Character versus Society

"Guys like us, that work on ranches, are the loneliest guys in the world. They got no family. They don't belong no place. They ain't got nothing to look ahead to … With us it ain't like that. We got a future. We got somebody to talk to that gives a [expletive] about us."

George Milton, Chapter 1

TEACHER NOTES

More

The Types of Conflict in Of Mice and Men

Analyze the citations from the novella revealing the types of conflict as they appear in *Of Mice and Men*.

1. How do these excerpts of conflict reveal the novella's theme? How do they reveal character? Explain and defend your ideas.
2. Write an analysis of Steinbeck's development of conflict between George and Lennie. What deeper truths may be suggested about these characters as a result of their conflict?

Weblink

To a Mouse, on Turning Her up in Her Nest with the Plough

Examine the Robert Burns poem that inspired the title of the novella.

1. What reasons would Steinbeck have for naming *Of Mice and Men* after the line from Burns's poem? In terms of Steinbeck's novella, who might be the mouse and the speaker? Give reasons for your ideas.
2. Which of the verses in the poem are particularly exemplary of the conflicts faced by Lennie in the novella? How? Provide reasons for your position.

EXTENSION ACTIVITY

Analyzing a Video

Students will watch and assess a video related to a component of the novella, and write an analysis of the video. An exemplary video analysis will meet the following criteria.

- Identifies the purpose of the video
- Identifies the intended audience of the video
- Describes how the content of the video is presented
- Summarizes the information and opinions presented in the video
- Analyzes the quality of the content presented in the video
- Assesses the effectiveness of the video
- Discusses the technical aspects of the video and whether or not these enhance the content
- Determines whether the images and graphics used in the video relate to the content
- Determines whether the video is easy to follow and understand
- Gives the analysis a clear and consistent purpose
- Organizes the analysis in a logical, effective manner
- Presents a strong, clear argument about the video
- Provides strong and accurate details to support the argument about the video
- Considers other perspectives on the purpose and effectiveness of the video
- Makes connections between the video and the novella
- Properly integrates quotations from the video
- Cites all sources used in the analysis

Introducing the Characters

Writers use both direct and indirect methods to reveal their characters. Good writers tend to rely on indirect methods of character development. Some writers comment on their characters' personalities from the **perspective** of other characters. These third-person omniscient or third-person limited points of view allow the reader to see into the minds of all or some of the characters. John Steinbeck takes a different approach in *Of Mice and Men*. He uses the third-person objective point of view. Third-person objective does not provide the thoughts of any characters.

Major Characters in *Of Mice and Men*

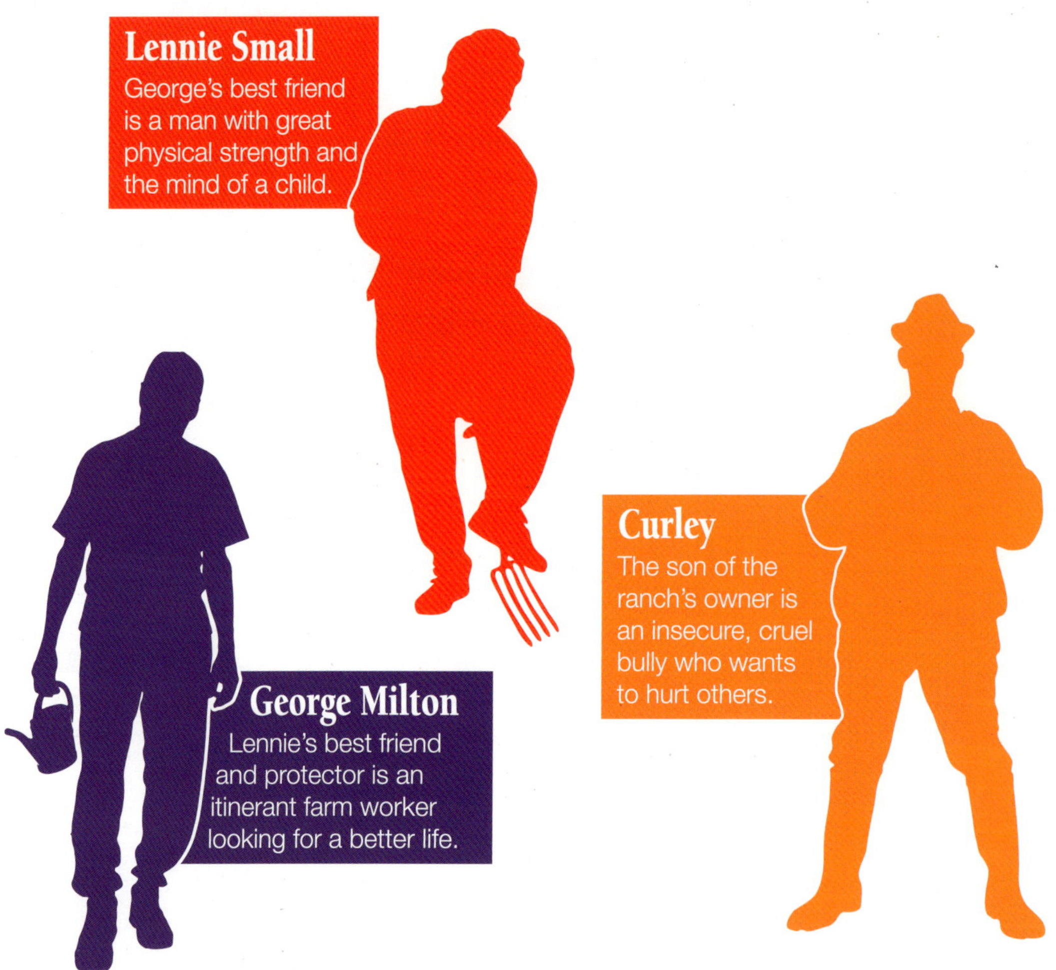

Most stories have a protagonist and an antagonist. The protagonist is the central character. He or she must resolve a conflict over the course of the story, and as a result, often develops as a character. The protagonist of *Of Mice and Men*, George Milton, faces the challenge of protecting his best friend, Lennie Small. He works to find jobs to help them both survive and make their dream of owning a farm a reality. By the end of the novella, George must deal with the **moral** dilemma of how to keep Lennie safe from Curley.

The antagonist is the character or force who stands in opposition to the protagonist. The antagonist of the novella, Curley, is a cruel man who bullies others to make himself feel important. He treats the workers badly, picks fights, and is rude to George and Lennie.

There are many different types of minor characters that assist in moving the plot forward. A dynamic character changes throughout the story, usually after facing conflict. A static character, such as Lennie, does not undergo changes. A flat character, such as Carlson, has only one personality trait, while a round character, such as Crooks, has a more complex personality.

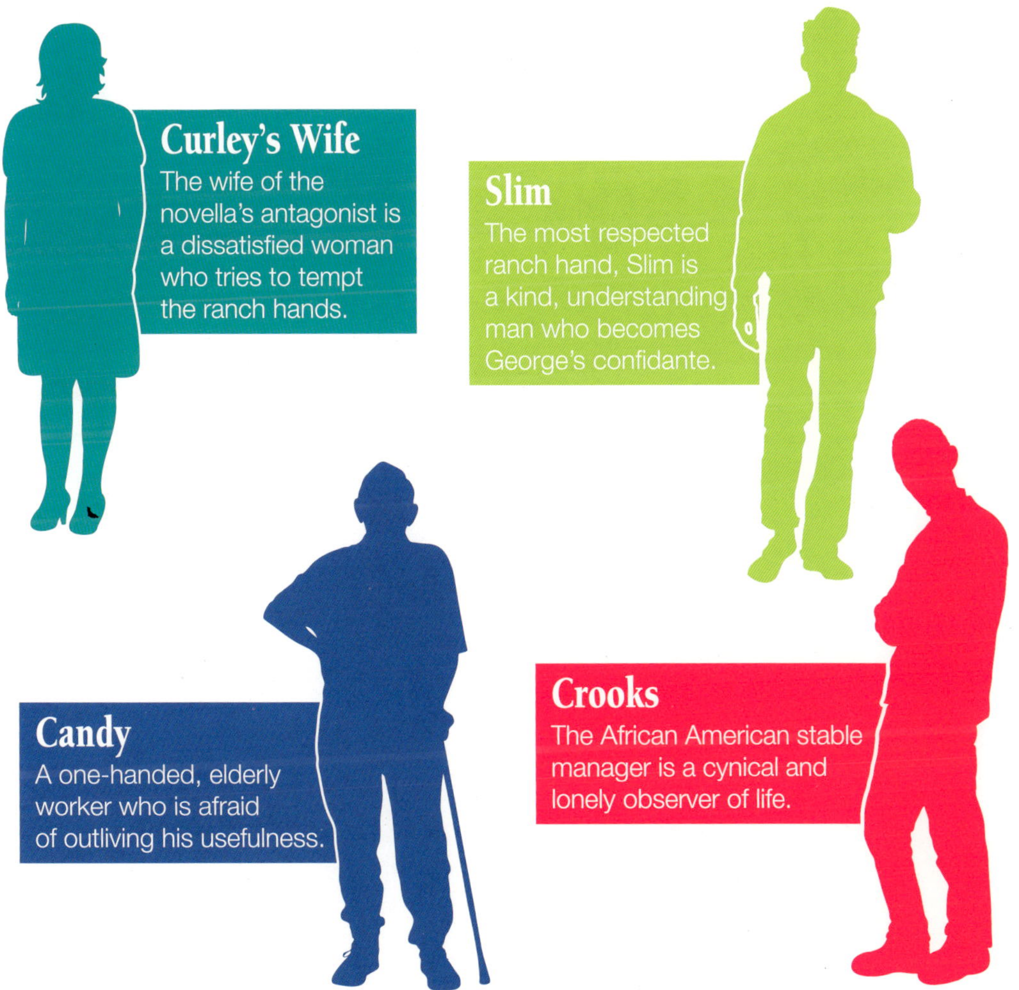

TEACHER NOTES

Video

***Of Mice and Men*, Act 1 Scene 1 Part 1**

Assess the performances and characterization of George and Lennie as they are portrayed in a stage play adaption of the novella.

1. What aspects of the actors' performances are most effective in the portrayal of the characters as they appear in the novella? Which aspects seem inconsistent or ineffective? Provide reasons for your opinions.
2. Is this stage play adaptation consistent with the tone generated by the opening pages of the novella? Why or why not?

More

Character Development in *Of Mice and Men*

Analyze the characters in *Of Mice and Men* using the descriptions on the character map and excerpts from each character. Then, choose a character and answer the following questions.

1. Which of the writer's techniques are most effective at revealing this character's traits? Why?
2. In what ways is the characterization of this character ineffective? What could be done to improve this character's function in the novella? Defend your ideas with evidence.

EXTENSION ACTIVITY

Creating a Literary Device Analysis Booklet

Students will analyze the author's use of a literary device in the novella, and create a booklet to present this analysis. An exemplary literary device analysis booklet will meet the following criteria.

- Defines the chosen literary device accurately and in detail
- Places the definition of the literary device at the beginning of the booklet
- Provides strong, specific examples of how this literary device is used in the novella
- Describes examples in detail, with quotations properly integrated
- Includes thorough analysis of the use, purpose, and effectiveness of each example of how the chosen literary device is used in the novella
- Arranges all pages logically
- Examples are organized chronologically
- Provides no more than one example and its analysis per page
- Creates a neat, well-organized, and attractive booklet
- Booklet is colorful and displays the student's creativity
- Uses illustrations to represent the chosen literary device and the examples of how it is used in the novella

The Art of Storytelling

Storytelling is a way to entertain, engage with others, teach, or communicate perspectives on society. A narrative, or story, is a series of events that is often logically arranged. When writing his or her story, a writer structures the narrative in a particular way. The writer uses different types of literary devices to create a distinct style and convey the narrative's overall message. In order to tell his story effectively, John Steinbeck structured his narrative, created a plot, and used a number of literary devices in *Of Mice and Men*.

Structure of a Narrative

Each narrative has a structure, which writers keep in mind when creating a story. The most common narrative structure, known as dramatic structure or Freytag's Pyramid, consists of five main components—all of which are used in *Of Mice and Men*.

Freytag's Pyramid

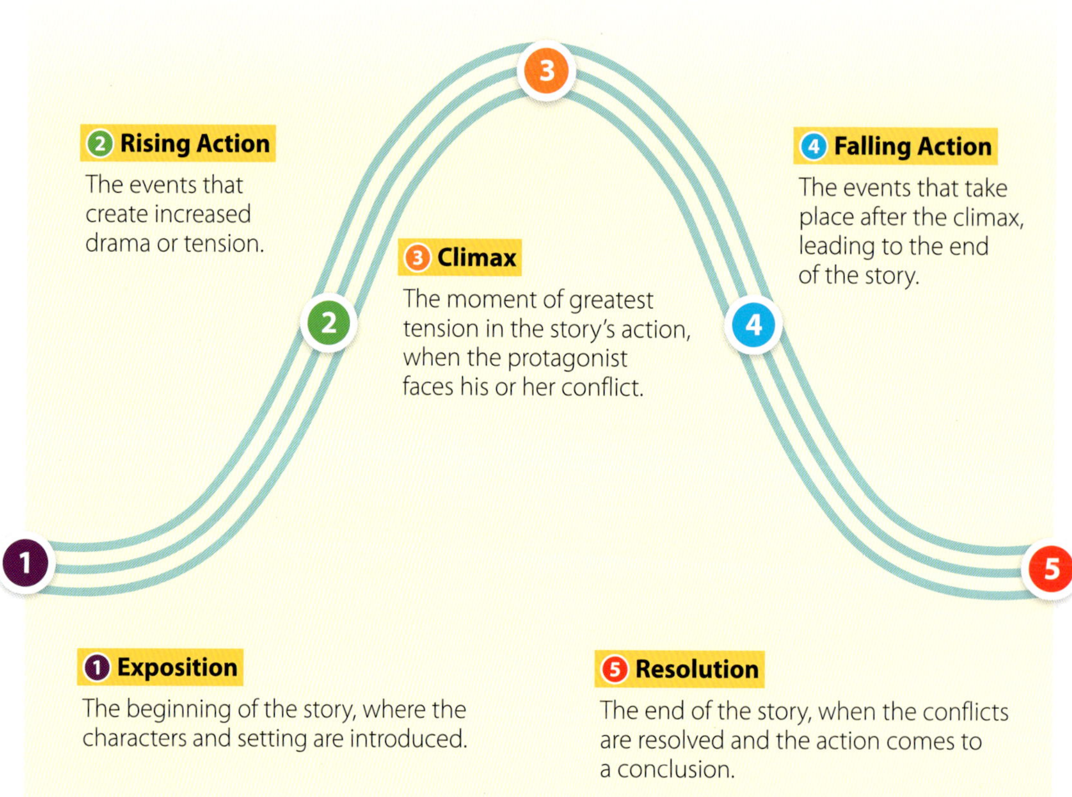

Plot

Every narrative needs to have a plot. Plot is the series of actions that propel the story forward. The plotline is the order in which events, or plot points, take place. These events build on each other and are organized in a logical manner. Each event causes the next event to happen, thus creating the narrative.

Plot Points in Chapter 1 of *Of Mice and Men*

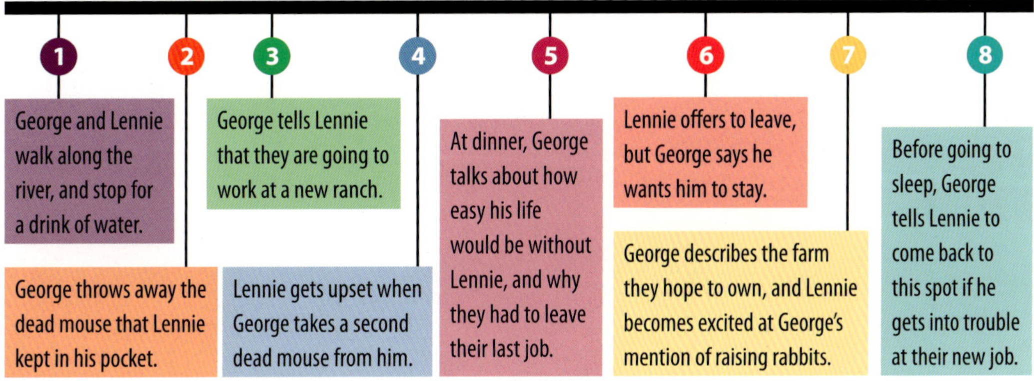

Literary Devices

A literary device is any particular feature of a work of literature that can be identified, studied, and analyzed. The two types of literary devices are literary elements and literary techniques.

TEACHER NOTES

Weblink

Six Tips on Writing from John Steinbeck
Examine selected advice gleaned Steinbeck's posthumously-published *A Life in Letters*.

1. In what ways is Steinbeck's advice about dialogue evidenced in *Of Mice and Men*? How do Steinbeck's dialogue choices enhance the novella?
2. Assess what the important message Steinbeck felt an "aching urge" to convey was for *Of Mice and Men*. Did he convey it effectively? To what degree? Explain your position.

More

Examples of Literary Techniques from the Novella
Analyze the author's use of literary techniques and how they contribute to the narrative of *Of Mice and Men*.

1. Choose one literary technique used in the novella. In what particular way did the author use this literary technique? Was it effective in its usage? Why or why not?
2. What arguments can be made for the use of your chosen literary technique in a text? If this technique were overused or underutilized, what effect might it have on an author's work?

Theme in the Novella

The theme is the underlying idea or opinion about the topic of the story. It is often a general, universal statement about life. The theme can be clearly stated or subtly suggested.

A theme is different from the topic of a novella. While the topic is the subject of a story, theme makes a statement about the topic. Theme can be expressed through the events that take place in the story, repeated ideas, and the lessons the characters learn. The theme of a story is often open to interpretation. A reader may have to examine many different aspects of a novella in order to form an opinion about its themes.

Values

Closely related to a novella's themes are the different **values** held by the story's characters. Values are revealed through the words and actions of the characters. Values often inform or become the basis of a particular theme in the novella. Sometimes, a character's values will reflect those of the writer. John Steinbeck's perspectives on social justice and the treatment of workers during the 1930s are the values that shaped his novella's themes.

Major Themes in *Of Mice and Men*

Of Mice and Men explores human nature and asks the reader to consider the moral issues presented in the narrative. Steinbeck created a story that leaves the reader questioning the forces at work throughout the novella. The major themes in *Of Mice and Men* are friendship, impossible dreams, and loneliness.

Friendship

"'You guys travel around together?' …
…'Sure,' said George. 'We kinda look after each other.' He indicated Lennie with his thumb. 'He ain't bright. … a good worker, though. … I've known him for a long time.'
Slim looked through George and beyond him. 'Ain't many guys travel around together,' he mused. 'I don't know why. Maybe ever'body in the whole [expletive] world is scared of each other.' …
'It's a lot nicer to go around with a guy you know,' said George."

George Milton and Slim, Chapter 2

George Milton

Impossible Dreams

"Sure, we'd have a little house an' a room to ourself. Little fat iron stove, an' in the winter we'd keep a fire goin' in it. It ain't enough land so we'd have to work too hard. Maybe six, seven hours a day. We wouldn't have to buck no barley eleven hours a day. An' when we put in a crop, why, we'd be there to take the crop up. We'd know what come of our planting."

George Milton, Chapter 3

Crooks

Loneliness

"S'pose you didn't have nobody. S'pose you couldn't go into the bunk house and play rummy 'cause you was black. How'd you like that? S'pose you had to sit out here an' read books. Sure you could play horseshoes till it got dark, but then you got to read books. Books ain't no good. A guy needs somebody—to be near him … A guy goes nuts if he ain't got nobody."

Crooks, Chapter 4

Secondary Themes

Secondary themes are those that are not heavily emphasized in the narrative. While it does not play as large a role as a major theme, a secondary theme adds another layer to the ideas presented by the story, allowing for a more complex narrative and deeper literary analysis. Examples of secondary themes explored in *Of Mice and Men* include **fate**, **discrimination**, the weak and the strong, and the nature of women.

TEACHER NOTES

Weblink

***Of Mice and Men*, America's Mirror of Fallibilities**

Evaluate the article discussing the variety of themes present in *Of Mice and Men*.

1. What was Steinbeck's intended thematic purpose for Curley's wife? Does she serve this purpose? Why or why not? Defend your position with evidence from the novella.
2. What statements might Steinbeck be making about the treatment of women in the 1930s through the character and behavior of Curley's wife? How fair is Steinbeck's portrayal of her? What evidence is there that Steinbeck sympathized with women?

More

Major and Secondary Themes

Analyze the author's development of themes over the course of the novella.

1. Choose a secondary theme from this spread and analyze its appearances in the novella. How does this theme first emerge? Which is the most poignant example of this theme in the novella? Provide reasons for your position.
2. What particular commentary might the author be making about life as a result of this theme's presence in the text?
3. Choose a major theme presented on pages 16–17. In what ways does your chosen secondary theme relate to this major theme? Does it deepen or detract from the major theme? How or in what way?

EXTENSION ACTIVITY

Creating a Symbolism Poster

Students will choose one of the other symbols listed on page 19 and analyze its role in the novella. They will then create a poster to present their analysis. An exemplary symbolism poster will meet the following criteria.

- Presents a clear purpose that is conveyed throughout the poster
- Shows an understanding of the concept of symbolism and the role it plays in the novella
- Provides an in-depth analysis of what the symbol represents
- Discusses the role the symbol plays in the novella
- Clearly indicates where the symbol appears in the novella
- Uses specific, detailed examples from the text to support the analysis
- Makes clear connections to the text
- Properly integrates all quotations
- Organizes the information in a logical, easy-to-read manner
- Includes high-quality graphics that relate to the symbol and effectively enhance understanding of the topic
- Features clear and concise writing
- Uses correct spelling, grammar, and punctuation
- Clearly labels items of importance
- Headings and subheadings are clear and easy to read
- Uses layout to creatively enhances the information
- Creates a poster that is attractive in terms of layout, design, and organization
- Shows a strong effort by the student

Symbolism in the Novella

Symbolism is a literary technique writers use to help convey theme. A symbol is often a tangible object, such as the farm, to which a writer lends deeper meaning. Other times, action or dialogue in the narrative can be symbolic of a specific idea or theme.

Symbolism gives the story's events, characters, and themes a universal feel. Sometimes, it sheds light on how the writer feels about specific concepts and ideas. When studying a work of literature, the reader can gain a deeper understanding of the story by identifying and analyzing the symbols used by the writer. If a reader has trouble identifying symbols in the novella, a good place to look first is the work's title.

Mice as a Symbol

Lennie's mice represent innocence and vulnerability in *Of Mice and Men*. The mice do not realize that there will be consequences when they bite Lennie. In the same way, Lennie's inability to fully comprehend the harm he causes others becomes his eventual undoing.

Lennie's Mice

Lennie looked sadly up at him. "They was so little," he said apologetically. "I'd pet 'em, and pretty soon they bit my fingers and I pinched their heads a little and then they was dead—because they was so little."

Lennie Small, Chapter 1

The Farm as a Symbol

George describes the farm that he and Lennie hope to buy as a kind of paradise that stands in stark contrast to their present reality. Owning their own farm would allow the men the freedom to determine their own futures. It is, in essence, the **American Dream**. This dream of a safe home and hopeful future would have been particularly powerful for an itinerant worker during the Great Depression.

The Farm

"'Go on—tell again, George.'
'Well, it's ten acres,' said George. 'Got a little win'mill. Got a little shack on it, an' a chicken run. Got a kitchen, orchard, apples, peaches, 'cots, nuts, got a few berries. They's a place for alfalfa and plenty of water to flood it. They's a pig pen—'
'An' rabbits, George.'"

Lennie Small and George Milton, Chapter 3

TEACHER NOTES

What Does the Farm Symbolize to These Characters?

Other Symbols in the Novella

Rabbits

When George describes the farm, Lennie's favorite part is that he will get to take care of the rabbits they raise. Rabbits symbolize Lennie's innocence and child-like nature. Lennie's enjoyment in petting the rabbits' soft fur symbolizes the actions that will later seal his fate.

Candy's Dog

Candy's dog symbolizes the idea that those who have outlived their usefulness will be cast aside. Candy fears that because of his age and disability, he too will be turned out of the ranch when he can no longer do meaningful work. As well, Candy's regret at not being the one to put down his own dog foreshadows the moral decision that George will soon be forced to make.

Lennie's Puppy

Lennie's puppy represents his own dependence on George. The puppy is helpless against Lennie's physical strength. The accident foreshadows the tragic event that is to come next.

More

What Does the Farm Symbolize?
Assess the author's use of symbolism in the novella.

1. Choose a character from the chart and analyze what the farm represents to him. Which character is the least poignant example of this symbol in the novella? Which character is the best example of this symbol? Argue your opinions with clear reasons.
2. How is this symbol used or reflected in the novella's themes? Illustrate the ways in which the author's use of language deepens or weakens the meaning of the farm as a symbol. Explain and defend your ideas.

Weblink

The Complete Guide to Symbolism
Examine the blog post discussing the usage of symbolism in literature.

1. Contrast and compare examples of analytical descriptions of feelings and sensory descriptions using symbolism from the novella. Which kind is more effective in the novella? Provide reasons for your ideas.
2. Should analytical descriptions play a considerable role in the language of a novella? Why or why not?

EXTENSION ACTIVITY

Writing a Book Review

Students will write a book review of the novella. An exemplary book review will meet the following criteria.

- Grabs the reader's attention with a creative headline
- Begins with an engaging lead to pull the reader into the article
- Introduces the title of the novella, the author, and the genre
- Provides a brief plot description that does not give away the entire story, and makes the reader want to learn more about the novella
- Supports arguments about the novella with accurate and detailed information
- Organizes the review and its arguments in a concise, clear, and logical manner
- Fits the format and style of a book review
- Follows the conventions of print or online journalism
- Demonstrates creativity in their approach
- Writes with a unique, engaging voice and perspective
- Provides fresh insight into the novella
- Provides an honest, authentic opinion on the novella
- Gives a clear recommendation on the novella, backed up by specific textual evidence
- Uses correct spelling, grammar, and punctuation

The Use of Language

The way in which a writer uses language is vital to any written work. Diction, or style of speaking, is used to enhance the messages of the narrative. John Steinbeck's use of language and diction in *Of Mice and Men* gives his novella a distinct feel, and helps create a believable and memorable narrative.

What Is Style?

Style is the way a writer uses language to tell the story. A writer's style consists of any number of literary devices used in the work, such as diction, syntax, imagery, and point of view. The author's choice of literary devices gives the written work a discernible feel and shapes its style. Many writers are known for their particular styles of writing. Style is used to present information to the readers and to convey the writer's purpose. Their purposes may be narrative, persuasive, expository, or descriptive. Some forms of writing, such as journalistic or academic works, follow specific style guidelines.

What Is Voice?

Voice is a writer's personality and form of expression. It is unique to the writer and is more specific than his or her style. While voice involves choices similar to style when considering how a work is written, voice gives life to written work.

In *Of Mice and Men*, Steinbeck writes with a descriptive voice that brings the novella's world to life. Each chapter begins with a vivid, detailed description of the setting. Some of his descriptions using sunlight are particularly poetic and meaningful. The beauty of these descriptions serves as a contrast to the harsh realities of life as portrayed throughout Steinbeck's narrative.

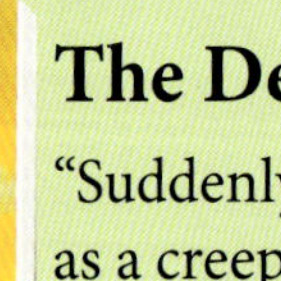

The Descriptive Voice of John Steinbeck

"Suddenly Lennie appeared out of the brush, and he came as silently as a creeping bear moves. The heron pounded the air with its wings, jacked itself clear of the water and flew off down river. The little snake slid in among the reeds at the pool's side. Lennie came quietly to the pool's edge. He knelt down and drank, barely touching his lips to the water. … When he was finished, he sat down on the bank, with his side to the pool, so that he could watch the trail's entrance. He embraced his knees and laid his chin down on his knees. The light climbed on out of the valley, and as it went, the top of the mountains seemed to blaze with increasing brightness."

Chapter 6

Words and Phrases Used in *Of Mice and Men*

A number of the terms used in *Of Mice and Men* are specific to the 1930s and may be unfamiliar to younger generations. Many of the terms have to do with the agricultural practices and social conditions of the era. Here are a number of words and phrases that appear in *Of Mice and Men* that illustrate the era, setting, and social conditions.

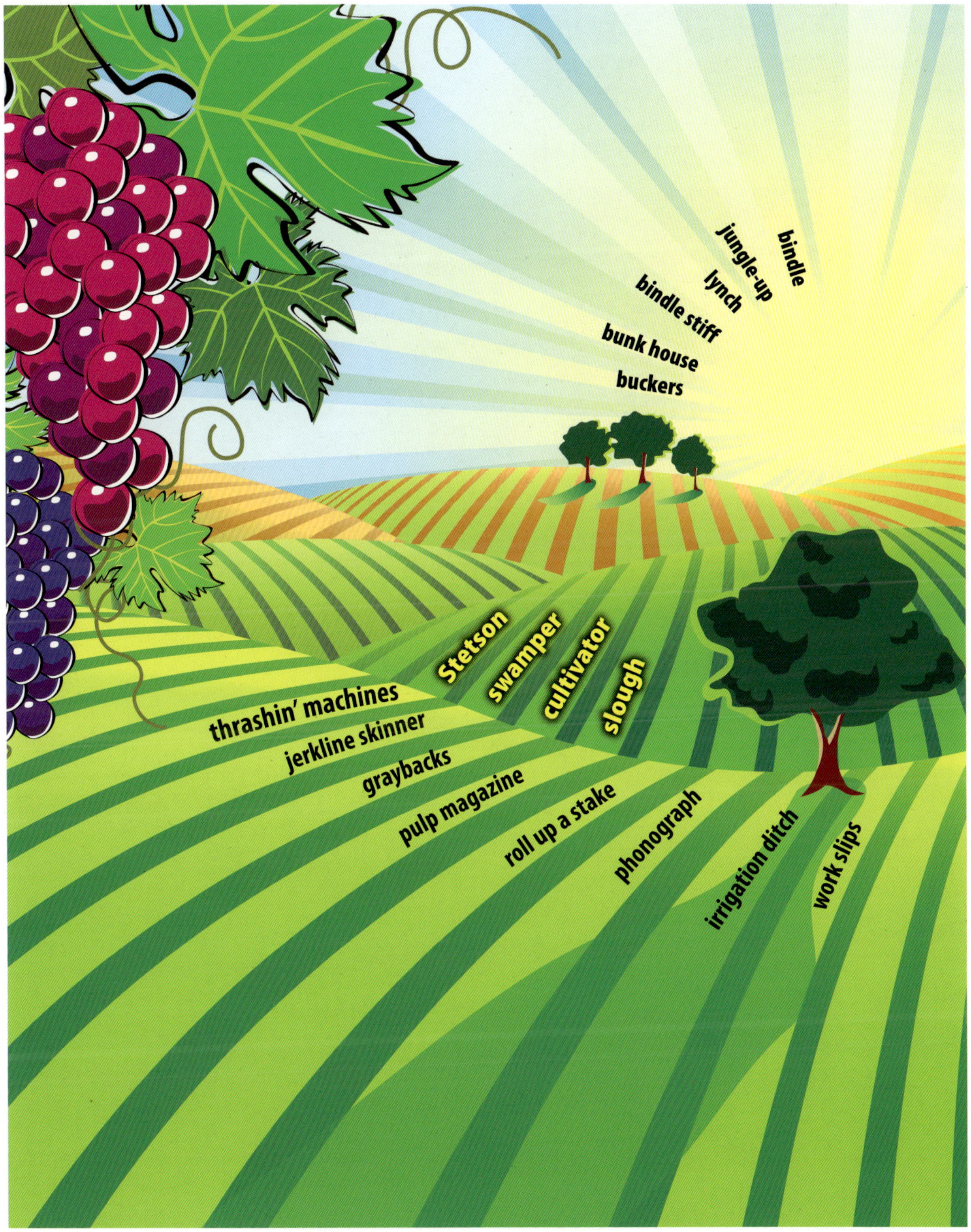

bindle
jungle-up
lynch
bindle stiff
bunk house
buckers
Stetson
swamper
cultivator
slough
thrashin' machines
jerkline skinner
graybacks
pulp magazine
roll up a stake
phonograph
irrigation ditch
work slips

TEACHER NOTES

Video

Mini Bio: John Steinbeck
Watch and analyze the mini-bio of John Steinbeck.

1. How are Steinbeck's intentions of creating *Of Mice and Men* as a play-novelette evidenced in the language of the novella? Which example of this evidence is the most poignant? Defend your response with clear explanations.
2. One of the speakers in the video suggests that George and Lennie's rich friendship compensates for the poor aspects of their lives. Is this an accurate statement? Why or why not? Cite specific examples of language in the novella to support your claims.

Weblink

What FBI Files Reveal about Hoover's War on Steinbeck
Examine the article written by Steinbeck scholar William Ray discussing the files the FBI kept on John Steinbeck.

1. How warranted was the FBI's investigation of John Steinbeck? In your opinion, how dangerous were the ideas and language in Steinbeck's works to the national security of the United States?
2. What reasons did J. Edgar Hoover have for lying in his response to Steinbeck's request to back off? Was this response ethical? Defend your responses with clear reasoning.

EXTENSION ACTIVITY

Analyzing Bias in a Document

Students will analyze the bias that exists in a document from a different historical time and place, and how that bias shapes the opinions presented in the document. An exemplary analysis of bias in a document will meet the following criteria.

- Identifies the main points presented in the document
- Offers an in-depth interpretation of the document
- Differentiates between facts and opinions
- Identifies the writer
- Presents information about the writer
- Assesses the writer's reliability
- Determines the goals for the document
- Considers and assesses the writer's perspective
- Determines the writer's intended audience
- Identifies when and where the document was written
- Describes the historical context for the time and place in which the document was created, and analyzes how this context might have shaped the opinions expressed in the document
- Infers political or societal influences that may have shaped the opinions presented in the document
- Determines whether the writer had first-hand knowledge of the topic or event, or whether they are reporting as a secondary source
- Determines the document's bias
- Infers what interests the writer might have had that led them to create this document
- Explores other sources related to the topic of the document

Impact of the Novella at the Time of Publishing

Of Mice and Men established John Steinbeck's reputation as a great American writer. Steinbeck, who was already well-known for works such as *Tortilla Flat*, became even more popular with his novella's publication. *Of Mice and Men* received many positive reviews, and critics claimed that the novella was at the same level of quality of his earlier books. This positive reception soon led to stage and film adaptations of Steinbeck's story.

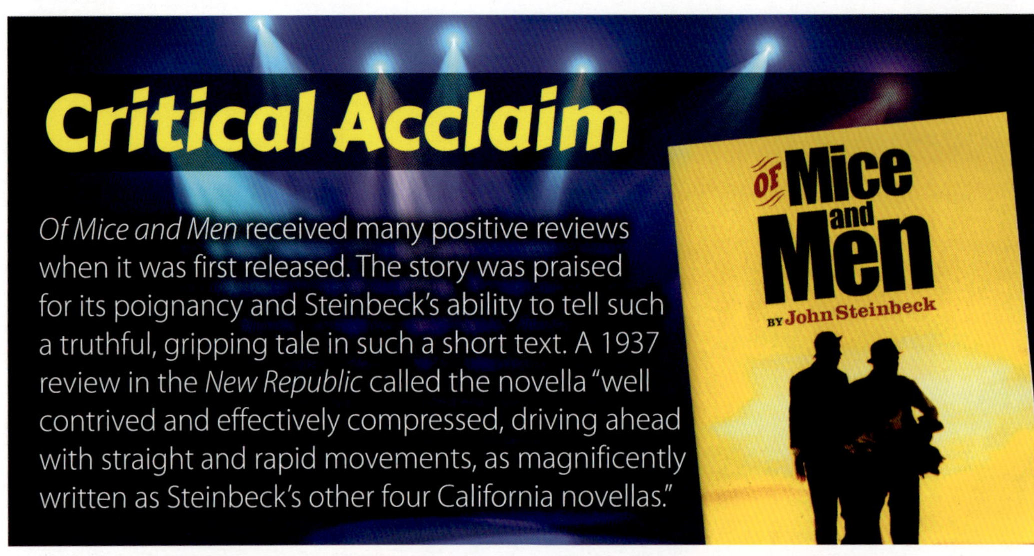

Critical Acclaim

Of Mice and Men received many positive reviews when it was first released. The story was praised for its poignancy and Steinbeck's ability to tell such a truthful, gripping tale in such a short text. A 1937 review in the *New Republic* called the novella "well contrived and effectively compressed, driving ahead with straight and rapid movements, as magnificently written as Steinbeck's other four California novellas."

Reader Response

Steinbeck fans could not wait to read *Of Mice and Men*. Approximately 117,000 copies were preordered before the book was released in February of 1937. The novella sold, on average, 1,000 copies a day in its first month.

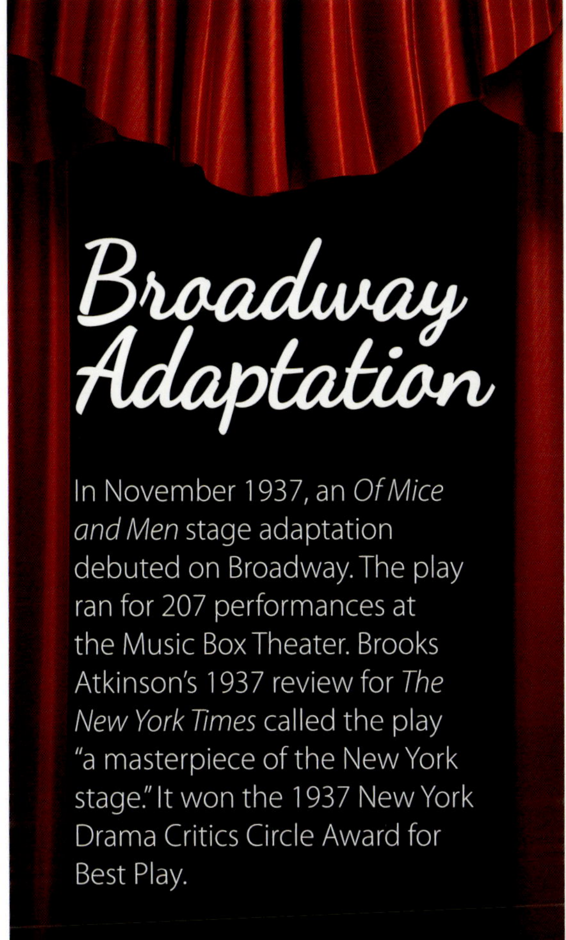

Broadway Adaptation

In November 1937, an *Of Mice and Men* stage adaptation debuted on Broadway. The play ran for 207 performances at the Music Box Theater. Brooks Atkinson's 1937 review for *The New York Times* called the play "a masterpiece of the New York stage." It won the 1937 New York Drama Critics Circle Award for Best Play.

Film Adaptation

In 1939, only two years after *Of Mice and Men*'s publication, the story was adapted for film. Burgess Meredith played the role of George, and Lon Chaney Jr. played the role of Lennie. The film gives more attention to the issues between Curley and his wife than in the novella, and is considered by some to be melodramatic. Some modern critics state that the film plays down the honesty and connection in George and Lennie's friendship.

A Celebrated Author

When Steinbeck was awarded the 1962 Nobel Prize for Literature, the presenter called him a "bold observer of human behavior in both tragic and comic situations." In his acceptance speech, Steinbeck said that writers are "delegated to declare and to celebrate man's proven capacity for greatness of heart and spirit—for gallantry in defeat—for courage, compassion and love."

TEACHER NOTES

Document

The Play: John Steinbeck's *Of Mice and Men* in a Production Staged by George S. Kaufman

Examine Brooks Atkinson's 1937 review of the Broadway adaptation of the novella for *The New York Times*.

1. Atkinson describes Lennie as having "pathetic helplessness." Is this a fair way to describe Lennie's character? How might a reviewer in 2017 describe a character such as Lennie?
2. What do you think Atkinson means by the term "rudely affectionate" when describing Lennie and George's relationship? Why would he choose these words instead of others? Explain and defend your opinions with evidence.

Video

John Steinbeck Gives Nobel Prize Speech

Examine the *Encyclopædia Britannica* entry discussing the African American Life during the Great Depression.

1. Compare what you know of Steinbeck with his description of Alfred Nobel in the video. In what ways are the men similar? How are they different? Provide reasons for your responses.
2. Using the internet, research what was happening in the United States at the time Steinbeck gave his acceptance speech. In what ways had "Man himself ... become our greatest hazard, and our only hope," as Steinbeck states? In what ways is this true today? How was this idea evidenced in *Of Mice and Men*?

EXTENSION ACTIVITY

Holding a Classroom Debate

Students will form groups and prepare arguments for a debate on a controversial issue. Exemplary performance in a debate will meet the following criteria.

- Demonstrates in-depth understanding of the topic and related information
- Presents strong, logical, and convincing arguments
- Communicates in a clear and confident manner
- Maintains eye contact
- Uses clear vocal tone and a reasonable rate of vocal delivery
- Uses respectful and appropriate language and body language
- Delivers arguments, evidence, and counter-evidence in an engaging and persuasive manner
- Supports each major point of an argument with several relevant and detailed facts and examples
- Connects all arguments to the overall topic in a clear, concise, and organized manner
- Presents the arguments and supporting evidence in a clear, logical manner
- Presents clear, thorough, and accurate information throughout the debate
- Addresses all of the opposing team's arguments with counter-arguments
- Identifies any weakness in the opposing team's arguments
- Constructs strong and relevant counter-arguments using accurate information
- Presents strong and persuasive arguments throughout the debate
- Summarizes the arguments in the closing statement

Impact of the Novella Now

In the 80 years since its publication, *Of Mice and Men* has earned its place as a classic of American literature. The novella is still studied in schools throughout the United States today. Its depiction of another time and its **poignant** message continues to resonate with readers around the world.

Banned Book

Despite its standing as an American classic, for decades *Of Mice and Men* has been challenged and banned for its language and content. According to the American Library Association, Steinbeck's novella was the fifth-most challenged book in the United States in 2000. In 2015, the Coeur d'Alene, Idaho, school board struck down a request by a parent group to remove the book from the ninth-grade English curriculum due to its use of profanity and "dark" content.

In a **2007** auction, a **first edition** of *Of Mice and Men*, owned by **Steinbeck's sister**, sold for **$7,768**.

As of **2012**, *Of Mice and Men* **had sold** more than **14 million copies worldwide**.

Of Mice and Men is one of the **10 most frequently studied books** in U.S. high schools.

New Film Adaptation

A film adaptation of the novella was released in 1992. It starred Gary Sinise as George and John Malkovich as Lennie. The two actors previously played these roles in a 1980 stage production of the novella. The film was praised for staying true to Steinbeck's story. *The New York Times* called the film "A recollection of a simpler way of life...."

Enduring Legacy

A 1992 article in *The New York Times* stated that *Of Mice and Men* has "withstood time's ravages with remarkable ease" due to its universal themes. The novella's themes can appeal to readers regardless of the era or place in which they live. Steinbeck's comments on human compassion and morality are seen as ideal lessons for young readers.

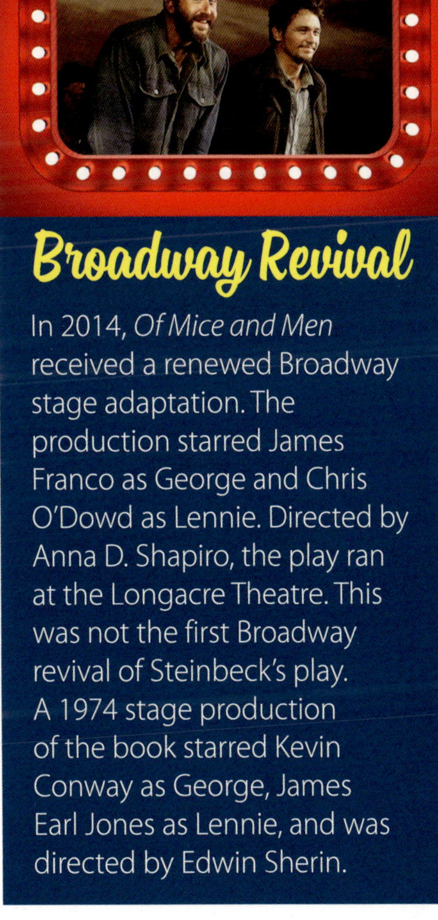

Broadway Revival

In 2014, *Of Mice and Men* received a renewed Broadway stage adaptation. The production starred James Franco as George and Chris O'Dowd as Lennie. Directed by Anna D. Shapiro, the play ran at the Longacre Theatre. This was not the first Broadway revival of Steinbeck's play. A 1974 stage production of the book starred Kevin Conway as George, James Earl Jones as Lennie, and was directed by Edwin Sherin.

TEACHER NOTES

Video

***Of Mice and Men* – The Final Scene Film Comparison (1939, 1992)**

Compare and contrast the final scene from the 1939 and 1992 film versions of the novella.

1. Think about the cinematography, pacing, and action in the final scenes of the two films. Which of the film versions is more faithful to the tone of the novella? Are there aspects of either film ending that seem inconsistent or ineffective? Defend your ideas with well-reasoned evidence.
2. Which of the two actors playing George is more effective? Which actor playing Lennie is the least effective? Provide thoughtful reasons for your responses.

Weblink

John Steinbeck's *Of Mice and Men* Survives Censorship Attempt in Idaho

Analyze Michael Schaub's article in the *Los Angeles Times* discussing the reasons community members in Coeur d'Alene, Idaho, wanted the book banned from schools.

1. Why might school teacher Brianna Cline's opinion about the presence of the N-word in the novella be a valid one? What arguments can be made against her statements?
2. What reasons might Steinbeck have had for including the offending words and phrases in the novella? Would the removal of this language from the novella have any effect on the authenticity of the book?

EXTENSION ACTIVITY

Creating a Timeline

Students will explore a topic related to the novella and create a timeline to present their research on historical events connected to this topic. An exemplary timeline will meet the following criteria.

- Includes the most significant events pertaining to the topic to be compared and analyzed
- Includes interesting events
- Uses accurate information for all events, including date, location, and major details
- Orders the events in a chronological sequence
- Describes each event with accurate, vivid, and specific details
- Presents the topic from three or more perspectives
- Inspires the reader to ask thoughtful questions regarding the events and perspectives presented in the timeline
- Uses correct spelling, grammar, and punctuation
- Presents the timeline in a visually attractive and striking manner
- Presents the timeline in a neat, organized manner that is logical and easy to follow
- Uses creativity to present the timeline in an engaging manner
- Effectively communicates the historical information relating to the topic
- Supports each event with reliable sources
- Expresses a clear purpose for creating the timeline
- Enhances the reader's understanding of the topic
- Includes a correctly formatted bibliography of all sources used to create the timeline

Perspectives on Disabilities and Inclusion

Of Mice and Men's compassionate message and unflinching depictions of struggle in a harsh world have haunted and humbled its readers in the decades since it was first published. At the time the novella was published, people with differing abilities were often marginalized and discriminated against. Steinbeck provides today's readers a glimpse into a time when there were no programs or legislation available for those with physical or developmental disabilities.

Rights and Inclusion of the Disabled Timeline

1700s — 1800s — 1900s

1792 Dr. Phillipe Pinel removes the chains imprisoning patients with mental illnesses at a Paris asylum.

1824 Louis Braille invents the alphabet for the blind that now bears his name.

1861–65 Thousands of American Civil War soldiers undergo amputations, bringing attention to issues for people with disabilities.

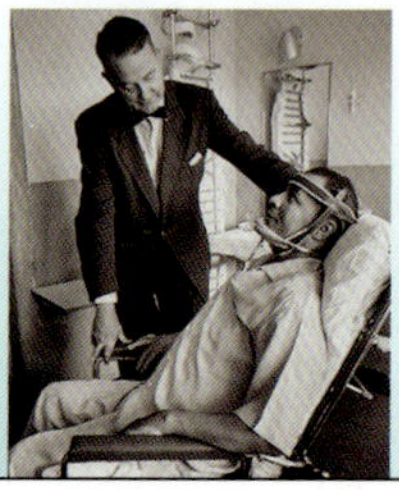

1918 The U.S. Congress passes legislation to establish programs that will rehabilitate wounded and disabled World War I veterans.

1935 U.S. President Franklin D. Roosevelt, the first president with a disability, signs the Social Security Act.

1948 Dr. Howard A. Rusk founds the Rusk Institute of Rehabilitation Medicine in New York to help wounded veterans returning from World War II.

For centuries, people with physical or developmental disabilities were regarded with fear and contempt, and often treated as less than human. It was not until the second half of the Twentieth century that the fight for legislation to ensure equal education and accessibility for people with disabilities was seen as a type of **civil rights** movement. While great strides have been made on this front in the last few decades, many argue that more can be done to improve **inclusivity** for all disabled people.

1975 The Individuals with Disabilities Education Act is signed. It legislates a guaranteed right to free, public education for all children with disabilities in the United States.

1978 The National Council on Disability is established as part of the U.S. Department of Education.

Today About 23 million working-age adults in the United States have some kind of disability. In 2015, the U.S. government spent approximately $143 billion to provide assistance to about 9 million disabled workers.

1900s

2000s

1950s The National Easter Seals Society and the Veterans Administration work to establish standards for accessible buildings throughout the United States.

1990 U.S. President George H. W. Bush signs the Americans with Disabilities Act. This legislation supports programs for all types of disabilities.

2004 The Administration for Developmental Disabilities funds the creation of Youth Information Centers to provide support and services for young people with disabilities.

TEACHER NOTES

Transparency–Timeline

Rights and Inclusion of the Disabled Timeline

Examine the historical, cultural, and contemporary contexts shown on timeline. Then, contrast and correlate its elements with the themes and events presented in *Of Mice and Men.*

1. In what ways can historical events, culture, and social mores influence a population's perspective on topics such as the rights and inclusion of the disabled? How might these elements have shaped the way a reader in the 1930s would interpret the novella?
2. How might the era in which John Steinbeck wrote *Of Mice and Men* have influenced the novella's themes and settings? Where in the novella is this most evident? Explain your reasoning.
3. Which current events, changes in laws, new ideas, or political discussions are shaping the rights and inclusion of the disabled today? How is inclusiveness improving? In what ways is it not?
4. How might current events and present perspectives affect the way a reader interprets the topics of disabilities and the rights of persons with disabilities as they are depicted in the novella? Why is it important for readers to understand the era and context in which a novella is written?

EXTENSION ACTIVITY

Writing a Comparative Essay

Students will compare two literary devices used in the novella, and then write a comparative essay based on their analysis. An exemplary comparative essay will meet the following criteria.

- Consists of a one-paragraph introduction, three body paragraphs, and a one-paragraph conclusion
- Introduction includes an engaging lead statement about the topic of the essay, more detailed information about the novella, and a one-sentence thesis that specifically states the essay's argument
- Body paragraphs include a topic sentence that refers to the thesis and how the idea appears in the novella, a supporting sentence that points to this part of the novella, textual evidence of this idea from the novella, and analysis of this evidence
- Body paragraphs end with a transition to the next paragraph
- Conclusion refers to the topic of the essay and the three points presented in the body paragraphs, and restates the thesis
- Provides a thorough analysis of the literary devices in question
- Cites strong and thorough textual evidence to support analysis of what the novella says explicitly
- Presents a clear, specific thesis that indicates a high level of critical engagement
- Organizes ideas in a logical manner
- Communicates arguments in a clear, effective manner
- Properly integrates all quotations
- Correctly cites all sources used
- Correctly formats bibliography

Writing a Comparative Essay

Of Mice and Men is brought to life with memorable characters, vivid settings, and poignant themes. After studying the novella, write a comparative essay to explore how two literary devices are used in *Of Mice and Men*. This could be a comparison of characters, themes, symbols, or settings. To write a comparative essay, you will need to formulate an argument. Your argument should clearly state how you feel your compared elements are similar or different. Support your argument with sufficient evidence from the novella and valid reasoning.

How to Analyze and Compare Characters

Use the chart to guide your comparison of two characters in *Of Mice and Men*.

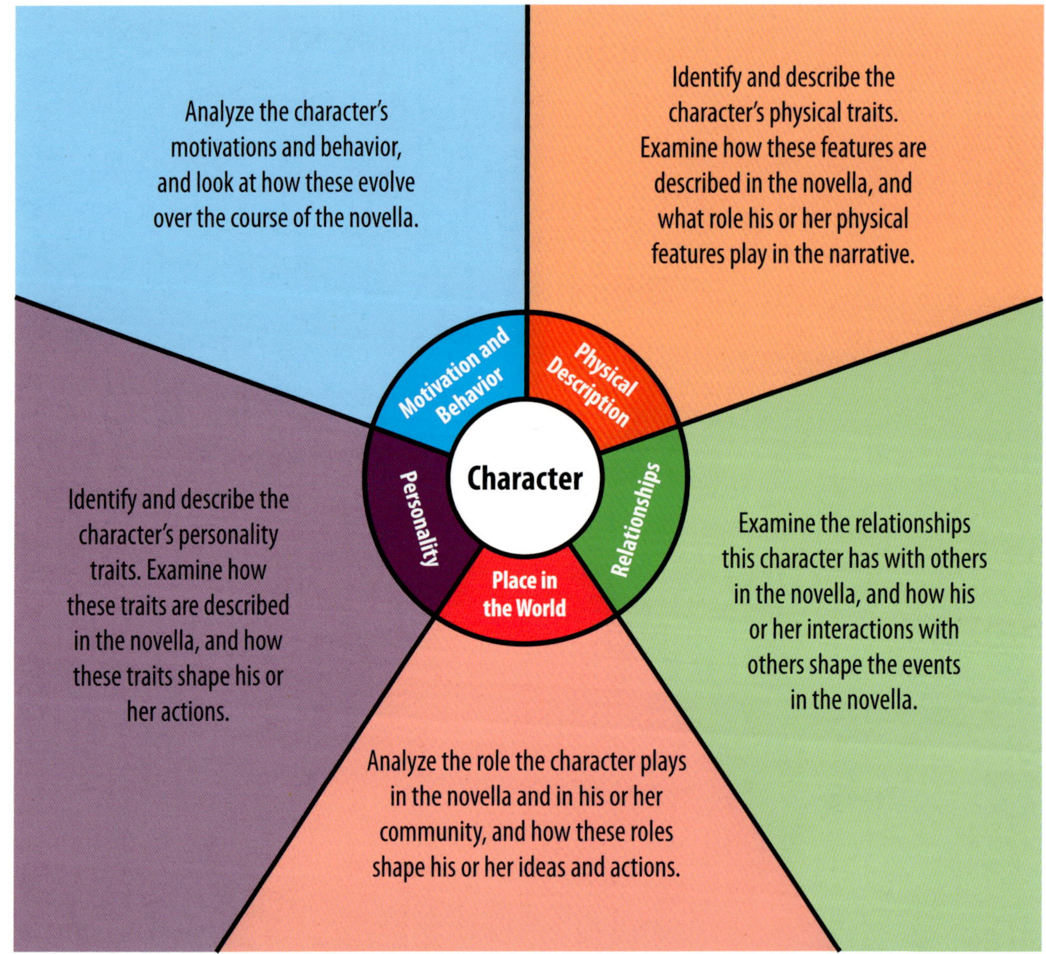

Comparing George Milton and Curley

George Milton

Personality
- Smart
- Protective
- Hard working
- Honest
- Blunt
- Moody at times
- Thoughtful

Place in the World
- Itinerant farm worker
- Does not have a home
- Working class
- Strives to find security

Motivation and Behavior
- Works to create a better life
- Protects Lennie at all costs
- Dreams of owning his own farm
- Avoids conflict if possible
- Stands up to bullies
- Believes he and Lennie are better off because they have each other

Relationships
- Lennie's protector and best friend
- Does not have living family
- Friend to Slim
- Gets along well with others

Physical Description
- Small stature
- Dark hair
- Restless eyes
- Sharp features
- Physically strong
- Wears denim

Curley

Place in the World
- Has a high standing on the ranch because he is the boss's son
- Tries to prove he is stronger than the others

Physical Description
- Thin and short
- Curly hair and brown eyes
- Mean-looking
- Wears high-heeled boots and one work glove

Motivation and Behavior
- Picks on the weak and powerless
- Insecure
- Needs to make himself appear stronger
- Always looking to start a fight for no apparent reason

Relationships
- The son of the boss
- Married
- Does not get along with the ranch workers

Personality
- A bully
- Impulsive
- Aggressive
- Jealous and possessive
- Mean-spirited

TEACHER NOTES

Transparency–Chart

Questions for Character Analysis

Analyze how specific character features, such as conflicts, motivations, relationships, place in the world, and personality affect the plot of *Of Mice and Men*. Cite strong and thorough textual evidence to support your analysis of what the novella says explicitly as well as the inferences you may have drawn from the novella's setting, themes, and symbols.

Quiz Answers

1. A
2. C
3. C
4. D
5. B
6. D
7. A
8. C
9. B
10. B

Key Words

American Dream: the idea that every U.S. citizen has equal right to achieve success, so far as he or she is capable, through self-determination

civil rights: a broad range of rights and freedoms guaranteed to all

discrimination: unfair treatment of a person or group, particularly on the basis of prejudice

fate: the inevitable outcome of something, thought to be predestined and out of a person's control

inclusivity: a policy of intentionally treating marginalized people or groups as equals

itinerant: traveling from place to place

moral: dealing with principles of what is right and wrong

novella: a story that is shorter in length than a novella, but longer than a short story; on average, a story that is about 20,000 to 50,000 words long

perspective: a certain point of view or position regarding a subject

poignant: deeply felt

social justice: fair, moral behavior or treatment in regards to the equal opportunities and rights of those within a society

values: an individual's standards of behavior and what aspects of life he or she considers to be most important

Literary Terms

antagonist: the character who stands in opposition to the protagonist; in some cases, the antagonist creates or represents the conflict that the protagonist faces

climax: the moment of greatest tension in the story's action

conflict: a struggle between two or more opposing forces, creating a tension that must be resolved

exposition: the beginning of the story, where the characters and setting are introduced

falling action: the events that take place after the climax, leading up to the end of the story

foreshadowing: a hint provided by the writer about an event that will appear later in the story

mood: the overall feeling that the narrative is intended to evoke within the reader

narrative: a logically arranged series of events presented for an audience; a story

personification: the attribution of human traits to something that is not human to give it a more vibrant description

protagonist: the central character in a piece of fiction who must deal with a conflict and often undergoes some type of change as a result

resolution: the end of the story, when the problems are resolved and the action comes to a conclusion

rising action: the events that create increased drama or tension

simile: a comparison of two different things using "like" or "as"

style: the unique way that writers use language to tell their story; this can include word choice, the use of imagery, and the length and organization of sentences

symbolism: a stylistic device using symbols to represent and intensify concepts and ideas

theme: the underlying topic, idea, or position in a work that is often a general, universal statement about life

third-person limited: the reader sees into the minds of some of the characters

third-person objective: does not provide the inner thoughts of any characters

third-person omniscient: the reader sees into the minds of all of the characters

voice: a writer's distinct personality and form of expression, as shown through his or her written work

Index

agriculture 7
American Civil War 26
American Library Association 24
Atkinson, Brooks 23

Braille, Louis 26
Broadway 23, 25

California 4, 5, 6, 7, 8, 22
Candy 13, 19
Cannery Row 5
Carlson 13
Chaney, Lon Jr. 23
children 27
compassion 23, 25, 26
Conway, Kevin 25
critics 22, 23
Crooks 8, 13, 17,
Cup of Gold 5
Curley 12, 13, 23, 29
Curley's wife 13

disability 19, 26, 27
discrimination 17
dream 7, 8, 10, 13, 16, 17, 18, 29
Dust Bowl 8, 9

East of Eden 5

farms 6, 7, 9, 12, 13, 15, 18, 19, 29
fate 17, 19
Franco, James 25
friendship 16, 23

Grapes of Wrath, The 5
Great Depression 8, 9, 19
Great Plains 7, 8, 9

itinerant worker 8, 9, 18

Jones, James Earl 25

laborer 7, 8
language 15, 20, 21, 24
literature 10, 15, 18, 23, 24
loneliness 11, 16, 17

Malkovich, John 25
Meredith, Burgess 23
mice 18
migrant 7, 8, 9
Milton, George 7, 11, 12, 13, 15, 16, 17, 18, 19, 23, 25, 29
moral 13, 15, 16, 19, 25
Monterey County, California 4

New York City 5, 26
New York Times, The 23, 25
Nobel Prize 23
novella 5, 6, 8, 10, 13, 16, 18, 19, 20, 22, 23, 24, 25

O'Dowd, Chris 25

plays 5, 23, 25

rabbits 15, 18, 19
ranch 6, 7, 8, 11, 12, 13, 15, 19, 29
Red Pony, The 5
Roosevelt, Franklin D. 26
Rusk, Howard A. 26

Salinas, California 4, 6,
Salinas River 6
San Francisco News 9
Shapiro, Anna D. 25
Sinise, Gary 25
Slim 13, 16, 29
Small, Lennie 7, 11, 12, 13, 15, 16, 18, 19, 20, 23, 25, 29
social justice 8, 16
Soledad, California 6, 7
Stanford University 5
Steinbeck, John Ernst Jr. 4, 5, 6, 7, 8, 9, 12, 14, 16, 20, 22, 23, 24, 25, 26
Steinbeck, John Ernst Sr. 4
Steinbeck, Olive Hamilton 4

Tortilla Flat 5, 22

United States 4, 9, 24, 27

veterans 26, 27

weak 17, 29
Winter of Our Discontent, The 5
World War I 26
World War II 5, 26

LIGHTBOX

SUPPLEMENTARY RESOURCES

Click on the plus icon found in the bottom left corner of each spread to open additional teacher resources.

- Download and print the book's quizzes and activities
- Access curriculum correlations
- Explore additional web applications that enhance the Lightbox experience

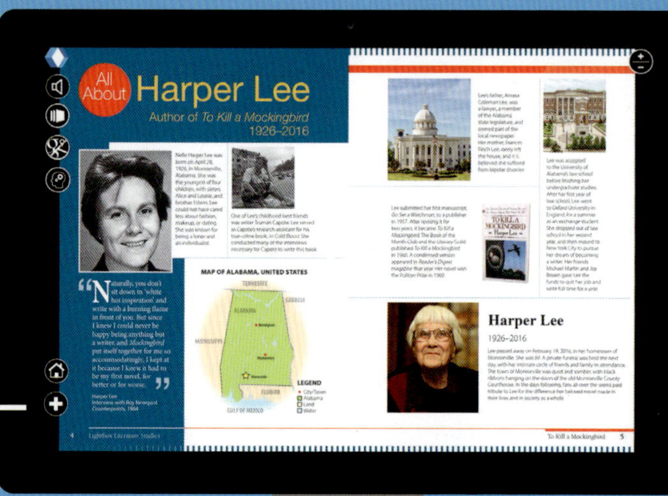

LIGHTBOX DIGITAL TITLES
Packed full of integrated media

VIDEOS

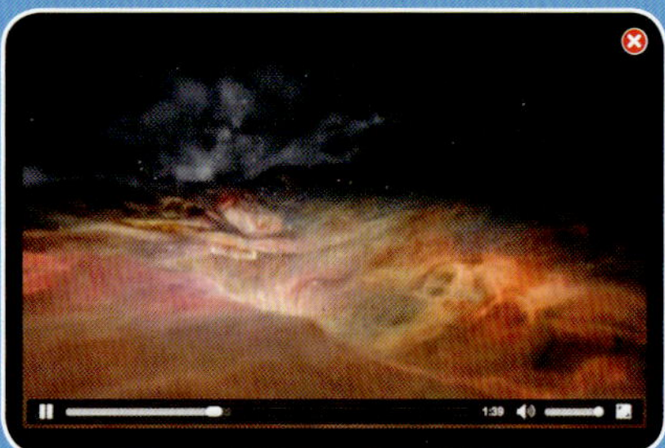

INTERACTIVE MAPS

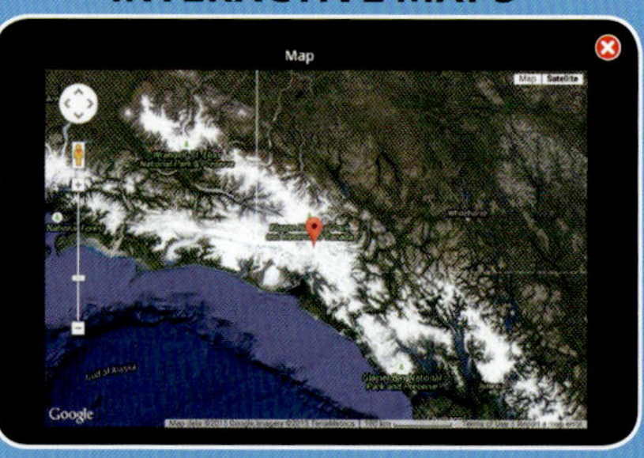

WEBLINKS

SLIDESHOWS

QUIZZES

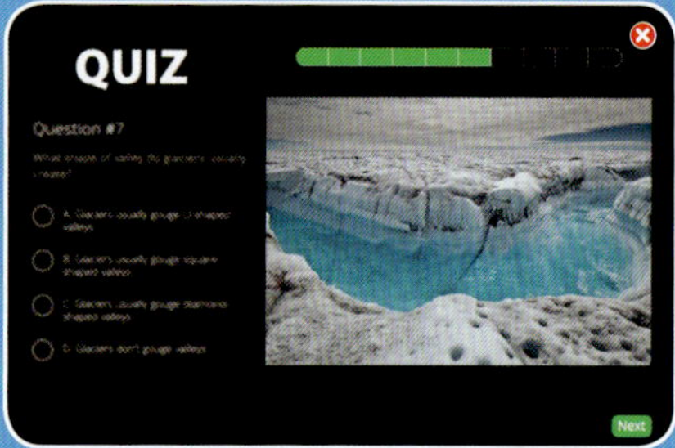

OPTIMIZED FOR

- ✔ TABLETS
- ✔ WHITEBOARDS
- ✔ COMPUTERS
- ✔ AND MUCH MORE!

Published by Smartbook Media Inc.
276 5th Avenue Suite 704 #917
New York, NY 10122
Website: www.openlightbox.com

042022
120422

Library of Congress Cataloging-in-Publication Data

Names: Whelan, Piper, author.
Title: Of mice and men / Piper Whelan.
Description: New York, NY : Smartbook Media Inc., [2017] | Series: Lightbox literature studies | Includes index.
Identifiers: LCCN 2016051610 (print) | LCCN 2017006302 (ebook) | ISBN 9781510520035 (hard cover : alk. paper) | ISBN 9781510520042 (multi-user ebk.)
Subjects: LCSH: Steinbeck, John, 1902-1968. Of mice and men.--Examinations--Study guides.
Classification: LCC PS3537.T3234 O4756 2017 (print) | LCC PS3537.T3234 (ebook) | DDC 813/.52--dc23
LC record available at https://lccn.loc.gov/2016051610

Printed in Guangzhou, China
2 3 4 5 6 7 8 9 0 26 25 24 23 22

Project Coordinator: Jared Siemens
Art Director: Terry Paulhus

Every reasonable effort has been made to trace ownership and to obtain permission to reprint copyright material. The publisher would be pleased to have any errors or omissions brought to its attention so that they may be corrected in subsequent printings. The publisher acknowledges Getty Images, Alamy, Newscom, Shutterstock, and iStock as its primary image suppliers for this title.